Copyright © 2014 Andrew Parker Davis

All rights reserved.

andrewparkerdavisis@gmail.com

ISBN-10:
0991667905

ISBN-13:
978-0991667901

1	We Must Do Things That We Don't Like	Pg 3
2	I'm Overcritical About The Things People Say To Me	Pg 4
3	Honesty Is Sweet	Pg 5
4	Almost There	Pg 6
5	Sometimes I Wonder What's Wrong With Me	Pg 7
6	Inspire Me Sweet God	Pg 8
7	**Leaf On Fire**	Pg 9
8	Stop Stop Stop! One At A Time!	Pg 10
9	Elegance	Pg 11
10	Give Me More!	Pg 12
11	**Yip Yap**	Pg 13
12	A Lovely Wind	Pg 14
13	Beautiful Stranger	Pg 15
14	It Got Dark	Pg 16
15	Think Twice	Pg 17
16	Really Shitty Lives	Pg 18
17	Lips Hold The Deepest Truths	Pg 19
18	Have You Ever Felt Disturbed?	Pg 20
19	**Pink Trashcan**	Pg 21
20	Evil Comes In All Shapes And Sizes	Pg 22

21	Little Holes	Pg 23
22	Entitlement Comes At A Price	Pg 24
23	The Most Destructive	Pg 25
24	What Kind Of Fruit Are You?	Pg 26
25	**Lonely Explosion**	Pg 27
26	My Body	Pg 28
27	Look At You Hourglass	Pg 29

Dedication:

To my mom, dad, brother, and Bob,
Kim, ABC, Jana, Mr. and Ms. Tran,
CPC Strategy, Lisa Berger, Liz Shipman, Juliana Snapper, Mr. Baldwin, Mr. Tibbs, Mr. Ojeda and last but not least Finest City Improv.

Thank you.

A Note From The Author:

There is no pattern to the poems in this book. Some are light, some are heavy, some are in between. They are yours to interpret as **you** see fit.

We Must Do Things That We Don't Like

We must do things,
That we don't like.
Things we don't like,
Help us realize,
To persevere,
Is to be alive.

I'm Overcritical About The Things People
Say To Me

I've been wonderin,

About your mumblins,

All day.

Honesty Is Sweet

Honesty is sweet,
Removes honey,
From my feet.

Honesty is sweet,
Lets me live,
As I please.

Honesty is sweet,
It also,
Rots my teeth.

Honesty is sweet,
Like a drug,
Guilt creeps.

Almost There

Almost there...
Just one hair...
Just...about...to get it...
Fuck yeah.

Sometimes I Wonder What's Wrong With Me

Sometimes I wonder
What's wrong with me?
It's getting so very
Hard to pee.

Inspire Me Sweet God

Inspiration dry.
Why?
Cry.
Bye.

Hi.
Die.
Why?
Inspiration dry.

Try.
Pie.
Why?
Inspiration dry.

Inspiration dry.
Why?
Fight.
Lie.

Leaf On Fire

Leaf on fire,
Nature's frenemy.
Leaf on fire,
Make room for history.

Stop Stop Stop! One At A Time!

Inside myself,
I can't keep up.
Shut,
The,
Fuck,
Up!

Talk to much.
Fun too fast.
What the fuck!
Please be still.

Breathe in deep.
Slow it down.
But but but!
Please be still.

Inside myself,
I want to kill.
Shut,
The,
Fuck,
Up!

Elegance

Elegance is overlooked,
It stamped ego in the history books.

Little snot nosed crooks,
Fate stabber drag fish.

Proper pink piper,
Right wrong life judge.

Fine fault Mary,
Lie more Gary.

Beauty nature's greatest trick,
Life's hidden foundation brick.

Give Me More!

Anticipation of something greater,
Makes for a great mental masturbator.

Hard to see what I'll lose,
When I can see what is due.

Yip Yap

Yip!
Yap!
Yop!
Yoop!
Which one of these rhymes with poop?

A Lovely Wind

A lovely wind,
Stirs the hens.
And then it's time for it to begin.

Crashing down with a thunderous applause,
Nature's jaws,
Slashing, lashing.

A lovely wind,
Stirs the hens,
And then it's time for it to end.

Beautiful Stranger

Beautiful stranger,
I wonder who you are.
Beautiful stranger,
Beside me at the bar.

It Got Dark

It got dark,
And I could not stop,
My dirty mind.

Oh well,
Who will mind?
It's not like they know what's inside.

Is your mind,
Like mine?
So much not said in life?

There's a world,
Where I live,
Inside my dirty mind.

Think Twice

Think twice about those you love,
Think twice about lips & drugs.
Think twice about every damn thing,
Except for the shit,
You don't need to think twice about.
Trust your damn instincts.
But think twice about it.

Really Shitty Lives

Really shitty lives,
They're everywhere.
So whenever you're down,
There's at least someone somewhere,
Who feels as bad or worse than you.
You're welcome.

Lips Hold The Deepest Truths

Lips hold the deepest truths,
The ones that speak and the ones that do,
Thieves, creeps and children too,
Lips hold the deepest truths.

Have You Ever Felt Disturbed?

Have you ever felt disturbed?
Like a germ on a worm?
Have you ever felt disturbed?
Like the victim of a curse?
Have you ever felt disturbed?
Permanently perverse?
Have you ever felt disturbed?

Pink Trashcan

Pink trashcan,
You elegant waste.
Pink trashcan,
I want to spit on your face.

Evil Comes In All Shapes An Sizes

Evil comes in all shapes and sizes,
Beware of the evil that surprises.

So close it will let you find it,
But you won't be able to define it.

So you try to live alongside it,
Get away or stay?

Play with evil or leave?
Let it let you bleed?

Change or be changed?
Let it grow or let it feed?

Or make it become your steed?
Which will be?

Little Holes

Little holes are the space,
That fill up the world.

The opposite of it,
Is holes.

The fuck you mean?
The absence of it.

The absence of it?
The fuck you mean.

The absence of knowing,
Is void.

That void,
Takes up space.

Entitlement Comes At A Price

Entitlement comes at a price:
Your soul.

Elegance comes at a price:
Your heart.

Beauty comes with small print:
What I am not is wrong.

The Most Destructive

The most destructive sounds,
Feelings,
Actions,
Beings,
Help us appreciate,
This moment.

What Kind Of Fruit Are You?

What kind of fruit are you?
Fresh or preservatives too?
What kind of fruit are you?
Sweet, sour, or blue?
What kind of fruit are you?

Lonely Explosion

Lonely explosion,
No one knows your name.
Lonely explosion,
I can feel your pain.
Created to destroy,
Then die again.
Lonely explosion,
What horrible pain.

My Body

My body is not,
A body that sings.
My body brings,
What my body brings.

Judge no body,
If it can't sing.
Cause our body brings,
What our body brings.

Look At You Hourglass

Look at you, hourglass.
One day your time will pass.

Look at you time passed,
Oh how you mask the past.

www.ingramcontent.com/pod-product-compliance
Lightning Source LLC
Chambersburg PA
CBHW070803050426
42452CB00012B/2480